ENDANGERED RAIN FORESTS

INVESTIGATING RAIN FORESTS IN CRISIS

by Rani Iyer

Fact Finders®

Table of Contents

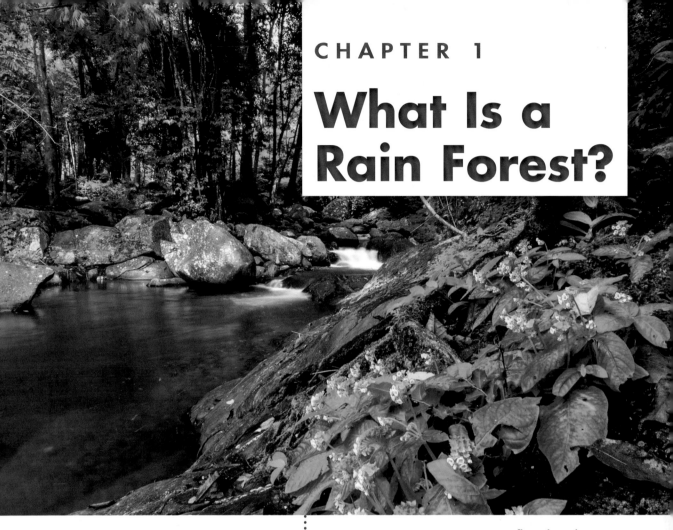

CHAPTER 1

What Is a Rain Forest?

A stream flows through a rain forest in Thailand.

Enter into the warm and colorful tropical rain forest. Different shades of green are everywhere. Sounds of howling monkeys and croaking frogs come from all directions. Cool rain begins to fall.

Rain forests are rich with life. They are home to a huge number of **organisms**. Flowers and vines grow among the trees. Birds fly above. Snakes slide around below. Insects occupy the forest floor. Every living thing has its own role in this **ecosystem**.

organism—a living thing

ecosystem—a group of animals and plants that work together with their surroundings

Rain forests are not just beautiful and full of life. They are necessary for the planet. Life on Earth depends on the rain forest in many ways.

Today rain forests all over the world are in danger of disappearing. People are cutting and burning down rain forest trees at a rapid rate. These actions destroy plant and animal habitats and have an impact on the whole planet. But people can stop the destruction if they are careful. Protecting and saving the rain forests takes a global effort.

a damaged part of a rain forest in Brazil

What's in a Rain Forest?

Most rain forests are tropical rain forests. These forests grow near the **equator**. They are wet and warm year-round. They grow in Central and South America, Africa, Asia, and Australia.

Rain forest trees grow to different heights. Canopy trees are big and tall, shading over the other trees. Emergent trees shoot out above the canopy. Sub-canopy trees grow right under the canopy. Below the sub-canopy are the understory trees. More plants grow along the forest floor.

Each layer of the rain forest ······ supports different life forms.

EMERGENT TREE

CANOPY

SUB-CANOPY

UNDERSTORY

FOREST FLOOR

FACT

Scientists believe the earth is home to about 8.7 million species. Only 1.2 million species have been discovered. It could take up to 1,200 years to record the rest of Earth's species.

..... a group of gorillas in the
        rain forest in Rwanda

Rain Forest Life

Only 2 percent of Earth is covered by rain forests, but they house 50 percent of all known plants and animals. Some **species** live only in one area and are found nowhere else on Earth. The termite-trapping pitcher plant grows only in one location in Malaysia. Mountain gorillas live only near the forest bordering Congo and Uganda. If one of these species dies out in one forest, it is lost forever.

equator — an imaginary line around the middle of Earth
species — a group of living things with similar features

CHAPTER 2
Rain Forests Are Important

... a young woman
working in the
rain forest in
Papua New Guinea

Rain forests are important to people around the world, even to those who don't live near one. They provide many necessities, including food, clean air, and water.

Living in the Rain Forest

Nearly 50 million people live in tropical rain forests. The Huli of Papua New Guinea, the Yanomami of South America, and Mbuti of Africa rely on the rain forest for survival. Their food, clothing, and shelter come from the rain forest. When human actions destroy or harm the rain forest, it threatens these people and their way of life.

The Mbuti People

For the Mbuti people of Africa, the rain forest is their home. Adult Mbuti are rarely taller than 5 feet (150 centimeters). Their height makes them well adapted to live deep in the rain forest. They live in small **nomadic** groups. For shelter they weave leaves and saplings into huts. They often use leaves for clothing. Families visit nearby villages to trade **bushmeat** and other rain forest products. In exchange they get tapioca, salt, and other produce. The loss of rain forests is threatening the Mbuti way of life. As forests are cut down for mining and logging, the Mbuti are driven away from their homes.

nomadic — traveling from place to place without a permanent home

bushmeat — meat from wild animals used for food

... Mbuti women

9

Rain Forest for Everyone

Most people live far away from a rain forest, but they use products from them every day. Many packaged products contain palm oil. Cookies, bread, soap, and shampoo all contain palm oil grown in or near tropical rain forests.

Many foods first came from in or near the rain forest. These include nuts such as cashews and vegetables such as peppers. Fruits such as pineapples, mangos, and avocados were once wild rain forest plants. If rain forests are not protected, the world could lose the wild relatives of these plants.

red mango fruit .....

.... A man harvests palm fruit used for its oil.

Chocolate at Risk

Chocolate is made from the seeds of cacao trees. These trees are native to parts of the Amazon rain forest. For centuries ancient peoples made a drink with cocoa beans. Beginning in the 16th century, cocoa farming spread around the world. Today cacao trees are grown on farms, mostly in Africa. However, many times the farmed trees die from diseases and pests. Scientists are studying the wild relatives of cocoa in rain forests of the Amazon. The wild plants may offer clues that could help protect all cacao trees.

cacao tree.........

Cool Planet

Rain forests help keep the Earth's temperature in balance. Most living things take in the gas oxygen. They produce the gas carbon dioxide. Carbon dioxide is also released into the air when humans use certain fuels. This extra carbon dioxide can warm the Earth too much. It increases the planet's **greenhouse effect**. Even a slight rise in temperature can cause changes in **climate** that put life on Earth in danger. During **photosynthesis** plants take in carbon dioxide. They then release oxygen back into the air. Large rain forest trees are best at taking in carbon dioxide. This helps to prevent **climate change** caused by too much carbon dioxide in the air.

Fog covers this rain forest in Thailand.

Rain Forest Rain

Rain forests help provide rain for the whole planet. Rain forests have more plants than other areas on Earth. All these plants absorb warmth from the sun. When plants warm, they release moisture into the air. Eventually this moisture forms clouds and rain falls. The rainfall refills rivers that provide water for plants, animals, and people. Many of the world's largest rivers flow through the rain forests. The Amazon **basin** alone contains 20 percent of all the freshwater in the world.

greenhouse effect—warming effect that happens when certain gases in Earth's atmosphere absorb heat and make the air warmer

climate—average weather patterns of a certain place throughout the year

photosynthesis—the process by which green plants make food using sunlight and carbon dioxide

climate change—a significant change in Earth's climate over a period of time

basin—an area of land around a river from which water drains into the river

Rain Forest Water Cycle

water falls down on Earth as rain

plants release water back into the air

CHAPTER 3

It Once Was a Rain Forest

Bare land is left in an area where rain forest once stood in Thailand.

Humans are destroying rain forests at an alarming rate. Experts say that about 80,000 acres (32,000 hectares) of rain forest are lost each day. All over the world, rain forests are cleared to make room for farming, mining, and building dams. Roads, homes, and cities stand where rain forests once did.

Deforestation

Deforestation is the large destruction of a forest by cutting or burning down trees. When a forest is clear-cut, all trees in one area are cut down. Other plants are also destroyed. Surviving animals must find new places to live. The cleared area is often used for farming. After a few years, the soil can no longer support the crops. Farmers must find new land. Sometimes forest can regrow in these areas, but the process is slow.

Slash and Burn

Sometimes farmers clear land by cutting down rain forest trees and plants and then burning the area. Sometimes this "slash and burn" process is used for small areas. Ashes from the fire provide nutrients for the crops for three to five years. Then the land is left behind. Some forest plants may be able to regrow.

Other times slash and burn happens too frequently or to too large of an area. The fires release harmful extra carbon dioxide into the air. There are then fewer trees left to absorb this gas. The smoke also adds to air and water **pollution**. After the land is left behind, the soil **erodes**, making it difficult for plant life to regrow.

pollution — harmful materials that damage the air, water, and soil

erode — to wear away

Haze covers an area of destroyed rain forest in Guatemala.

15

Farms and Plantations

Large companies buy parts of rain forest land all over the world. The land is cleared to plant crops such as palms, coffee, tea, and soybeans. In addition to the loss of rain forest, these crops need a lot of water. Water supplies run low. The crops also absorb less carbon dioxide than rain forest trees. Extra carbon dioxide builds up in the air.

Rain forests are also cleared to plant trees that are used to make paper. After the trees are cut down to make paper, the land is replanted again and again with the same tree species. This changes the soil and makes it more difficult for native species to regrow later.

a large soybean field next to the rain forest in Brazil

Orangutan Loss

Palm oil is used in food and to make cosmetics. In recent years the demand for palm oil has risen. To keep up with the demand, farmers in southeast Asia clear rain forest land to plant more palms. Orangutans depend on the rain forest in this area for survival. With no where to go, the orangutan population in this area has been cut in half.

an oil palm plantation

Ranches

Animals are raised for human food on ranches. In Brazil millions of cattle are raised on land that was once the Amazon rain forest. In addition to the loss of rain forest, cattle produce gas that fills the air with greenhouse gases. With less forest, there are fewer trees producing oxygen and cleaning the air.

Cattle now graze a field that sits where a rain forest was recently slashed and burned.

18

A rain forest is logged on the island of Borneo.

Logging

Logging is another land use that destroys rain forest. Loggers cut down rain forests trees. The wood is used for furniture, flooring, and building materials. It is also used for paper and paper products. Only certain tree species are cut down, but the whole forest is still affected. Losing one kind of tree makes it more difficult for species dependent on trees to survive. Fewer plants and animals can live in these areas.

Mining

Many rain forests grow in areas that are rich in metals, other minerals, and gemstones. Miners clear the rain forest and then blast the land open. Destroyed, forest cannot regrow on this land. When an area is blasted, dust particles remain in the air. This dust affects the breathing of people and animals. Soil erodes causing landslides. **Runoff** pollutes nearby rivers.

runoff—water that flows over land instead of soaking into the ground

Oil

Some rain forests grow on top of areas rich in oil. The oil is used to make gasoline and other fuels. Miners drill deep into Earth to reach the oil. Usually the rain forest is cleared before drilling can begin. The materials and process used to drill for oil can pollute the land, water, and air. Some of the oil is spilled or illegally dumped. This can be harmful to life in the area.

·········· an oil rig in a rain forest

.... a dam that is also used as a
public swimming pool

Development

When rain forests are destroyed for farming and
mining, nearby areas must be developed. Roads are
built through the rain forest to reach the farms and
mines. New cities are built for people to live close to
their place of work. **Dams** are built to collect and store
water. These dams destroy land and water habitats.

dam—a barrier built
across a river or stream
to hold back water

CHAPTER 4

Global Ripples

New planted trees begin to grow in an area that was deforested.

Loss of the rain forest causes a wide range or problems for the whole planet. It's more than a matter of losing trees and plants. Air and water are damaged. People, animals, and all life are affected.

Loss of Rain Forest Life

Rain forests are home to many species, including several that are **endangered**. When rain forests are destroyed, species lose part of their habitats. Species either do not survive the destruction or must move into a smaller area. Many times a species cannot survive in a smaller area and the population declines. Scientists say it's possible for some species to die out before they are even discovered.

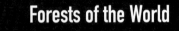
endangered—at risk of dying out

FACT

How long does it take a rain forest to regrow? When land in a rain forest is used for farming, the soil is only good for a few years. After farmers leave, a rain forest can take up to about 50 years to regrow. If some trees were left in place while the land was used for farming, rain forest can grow back in 20 years.

·········· Areas of tropical rain forest are colored in bright green.

Forests of the World

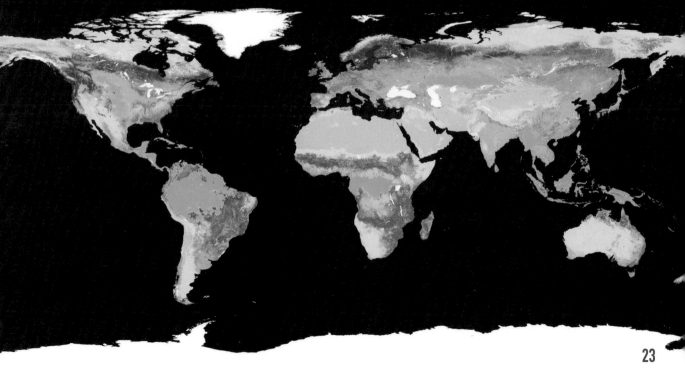

A Warmer Planet

Loss of rain forest also affects the world's climate. When old, large trees are cut down, they release carbon dioxide into the air. Every year tons of carbon is released into the air during deforestation. Carbon dioxide and other harmful gases are also released when people drive cars and use electricity. With the loss of so many trees, there are fewer of them to absorb this excess carbon dioxide.

Carbon dioxide and other harmful gases become trapped in the air. These gases cause Earth's temperature to rise. Warmer temperatures on Earth can cause polar ice to melt, areas to flood, and disrupt entire ecosystems.

These dead fish are one result of drought caused by Amazon deforestation.

Less Rainfall

Rain forest trees play an important role in Earth's water cycle. They add water to the atmosphere. This helps to form clouds that make rain. The more rain forest trees are cut down, the less moisture is released into the air. Less water is available to make rain. Less rain can cause drought and even more rain forest life to die.

Less rainfall affects life outside of the rain forest too. Moisture created by the rain forest travels around the globe. When Earth loses rain forest trees, there's less rainfall across the entire planet. This can lead to **droughts**.

drought — a long period of weather with little or no rainfall

This part of the Amazon River has dried up.

CHAPTER 5

Saving the Rain Forest

People around the world are working together to save the rain forests. Several organizations are dedicated to preserving this important ecosystem. What needs to happen to keep the rain forests from disappearing? People who study rain forests believe that governments, scientists, and citizens need to work together.

Forest Regrowth

With the right protection and support, smaller cleared areas can regrow. Scientists are working to help some areas grow back. It takes several years and there is often less life than the original forests. But the more plants that regrow the cleaner air will be.

Ecotourism

Ecotourism programs can help protect the rain forest and provide for people who live in them. These tours of delicate areas do not disturb the land. The money charged goes toward supporting and protecting the forest. Ecotourism also helps local residents by employing them as guides.

•••••••• tourists view the rain forest in Costa Rica

Loquillo Research Station

For 30 years scientists have carefully studied the rain forest at the Loquillo Long-Term Ecological Research station (LUQ) in Puerto Rico. The studies show that rain forests recover faster from natural changes than from the damage caused by humans. Scientists also study the ways rain forests impact human life.

Research and Studies

Scientists maintain permanent plots in rain forests to study the many organisms. Several ongoing, long-term studies will give scientists clues about how rain forests adjust to climate changes.

A scientist measures a large Rafflesia flower in the rain forest on the island of Borneo.

Everyone Can Help

Most people do not live near a rain forest, but their choices always have an impact on the environment. Here are some things people can do that will help protect rain forests.

Use less paper and recycle the paper after it is used. Write on the other side of paper before throwing it away. Buy recycled paper.

Buy food, including meat, from local farmers. This will stop support for food produced on farms created by deforestation. Also avoid buying products that contain palm oil.

Avoid buying new furniture made of rosewood, ebony, or mahogany. These woods are obtained from tropical rain forest.

Walk or bike to nearby places instead of driving. This helps keep the air clean.

Research and learn more about rain forests. Find a trusted organization to donate money to or find another way to help.

Rain forests are in a lot of trouble. But there is still hope. When people work together and everyone does their part, damage can be reversed. The remaining rain forests will be protected. The entire planet will benefit.

Bike riding rather than driving is one way to help keep the Earth clean.

29

Glossary

basin (BAY-suhn)—an area of land around a river from which water drains into the river

bushmeat (BUSH-meet)—meat from wild animals used for food

climate (KLY-muht)—average weather patterns of a certain place throughout the year

climate change (KLY-muht CHAYNJ)—a significant change in Earth's climate over a period of time

dam (DAM)—a barrier built across a river or stream to hold back water

drought (DROUT)—a long period of weather with little or no rainfall

ecosystem (EE-koh-sis-tuhm)—a group of animals and plants that work together with their surroundings

endangered (in-DAYN-juhrd)—at risk of dying out

equator (i-KWAY-tuhr)—an imaginary line around the middle of Earth

erode (i-ROHD)—to wear away

greenhouse effect (GREEN-houss uh-FEKT)—warming effect that happens when certain gases in Earth's atmosphere absorb heat and make the air warmer

nomadic (noh-MAD-ik)—traveling from place to place without a permanent home

organism (OR-guh-niz-uhm)—a living thing

photosynthesis (foh-toh-SIN-thuh-siss)—the process by which green plants make food using sunlight and carbon dioxide

pollution (puh-LOO-shuhn)—harmful materials that damage the air, water, and soil

runoff (ruhn-AWF)—water that flows over land instead of soaking into the ground

species (SPEE-sheez)—a group of living things with similar features

Critical Thinking Using the Common Core

1. How is life changing for people who live in rain forests? What adaptations and changes to their lives must they make? How is this different from what people who live outside of rain forests are experiencing? (Key Idea and Details)

2. To best protect the rain forest, what problem affecting it do you think must be solved first? Use information from the text and other sources to support your answer. (Integration of Knowledge and Ideas)

3. Reread page 6 and study the photograph and labels. What types of rain forest life do you think are best suited for each layer? (Craft and Structure)

Read More

Benoit, Peter. *Tropical Rain Forests*. True Books. New York: Children's Press, 2011.

Greenwood, Elinor. *Rain Forest*. DK Eye Wonder. New York: DK Publishing, 2013.

Moore, Heidi. *Rain Forest Food Chains*. Protecting Food Chains. Chicago: Heinemann Library, 2011.

Internet Sites

FactHound offers a safe, fun way to find Internet sites related to this book. All of the sites on FactHound have been researched by our staff.

Here's all you do:

Visit *www.facthound.com*

Type in this code: 9781491420393

Super-cool stuff! Check out projects, games and lots more at **www.capstonekids.com**

Index

ENDANGERED RAIN FORESTS

INVESTIGATING RAIN FORESTS IN CRISIS

An array of colorful life lives within the lush green walls of the rain forests. But these beautiful ecosystems and the organisms within them are quickly vanishing. Discover what human activity is doing to destroy this valuable habitat and what steps everyone can take to better protect this part of our endangered Earth.

ENDANGERED EARTH

Earth provides us with resources we could not live without. But our use of these resources and other actions are causing harm to the planet. Learn how your actions can help better protect our Earth and the resources we receive from it.

Titles in this set:

RL: 3-4 IL: 3-6

ISBN 978-1-4914-2214-4

90000

capstone
press

a capstone imprint
capstoneclassroom.com

9 781491 422144